the Gift of an Angel

the Gift of an Angel

is dedicated to Jim. — MR

© 1997, 2000, 2007 by
Marianne Richmond Studios, Inc.

LCCN: 2007903350

Marianne Richmond Studios, Inc.
3900 Stinson Boulevard NE
Minneapolis, MN 55421

www.mariannerichmond.com

ISBN 10: 1-934082-13-9
ISBN 13: 978-1-934082-13-3

Illustrations by Marianne Richmond

Book design by Sara Dare Biscan

Printed in China

First Printing

Also available from author & illustrator
Marianne Richmond:

The Gift of a Memory
Hooray for You!
The Gifts of Being Grand
I Love You So...
Dear Daughter
Dear Son
Dear Granddaughter
Dear Grandson
My Shoes Take Me Where I Want to Go
Fish Kisses and Gorilla Hugs
Happy Birthday to You!

Plus, she now offers the *Simply Said...* and
Smartly Said... mini book titles
for all occasions.

To learn more about Marianne's products,
please visit
www.mariannerichmond.com

For every child, there is an angel

hand-chosen in heaven above

and sent on a star to earth below

to protect, to teach, to love.

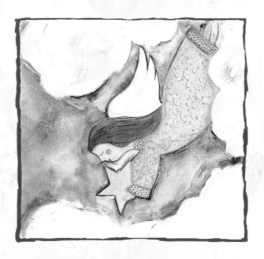

To *Meredith & Billy*

From *Mom & Roy*

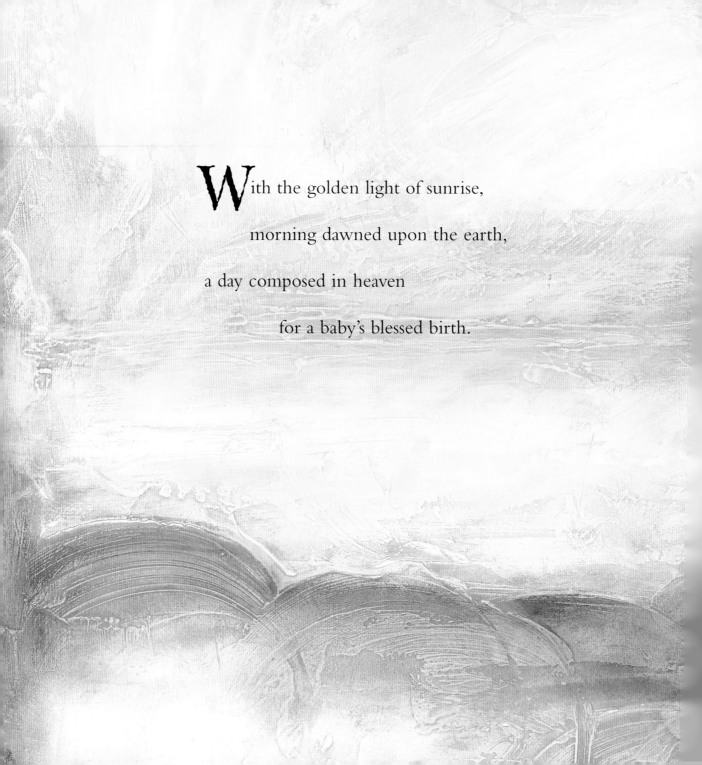

With the golden light of sunrise,

morning dawned upon the earth,

a day composed in heaven

for a baby's blessed birth.

Gentle color erased night's shadows.

Warm breezes nudged the world awake.

Bees and butterflies began to play,

as sunshine kissed the lake.

All things living danced in harmony

to the melody of love,

as expectant hearts prepared to greet

their dear child from above.

Amidst all this earthly ardor,

heaven stirred with anticipation,

as God tended to the special gift

for His miracle of creation.

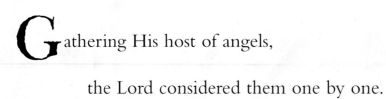

Gathering His host of angels,

the Lord considered them one by one.

"I need a volunteer," He said,

"to watch over this daughter or son.

"I've created a child so unique,

yet so needy of guidance and care.

I want to insure an angel

will for this child be there."

Then a beautiful angel with demeanor

always gentle, always mild,

accepted the Lord's invitation

to be guardian of the child.

Pensively, the angel asked,

"For this family, what can I do?

Aren't the parents you've chosen capable?

Won't they watch this child for you?"

"They will, my angel," said the Lord.

"But they can't be everywhere.

That's why I wish to give to them

my constant loving care.

"Your role in the child's life,

will gently unfold with the days.

You'll be a protector, keeper, friend . . .

and wise teacher of life's ways.

"You'll inspire the child to explore

as only a little child can,

with wide-eyed wonder and innocence,

with impulsive abandon.

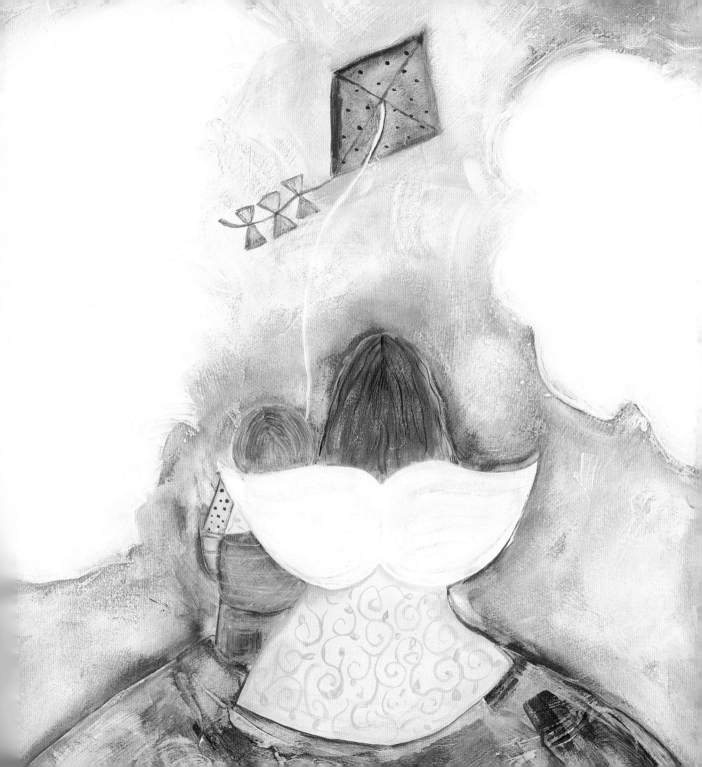

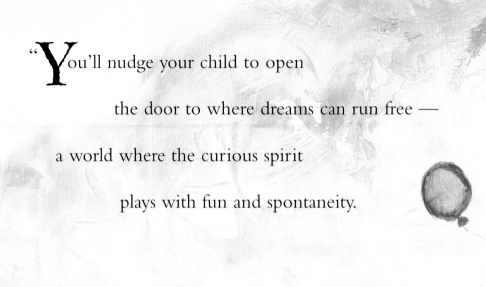

"You'll nudge your child to open

the door to where dreams can run free —

a world where the curious spirit

plays with fun and spontaneity.

"A place where a child can play pretend

with pirates, fairies and kings,

living on high seas and in strong castles

orchestrating awesome, imaginative things.

"And you'll lead the child down paths

filled with wonders of everyday —

a pudgy caterpillar, a plump bumblebee,

a butterfly meandering her way.

"You'll bestow on this family the wonder

that lets parents see through child's eyes,

helping them recapture the innocence

and moments of sweet surprise.

"Through you, they'll know heaven's goodness,

gentle peace that comes with love.

Days will be radiant and nights be filled

with quiet harmony from above."

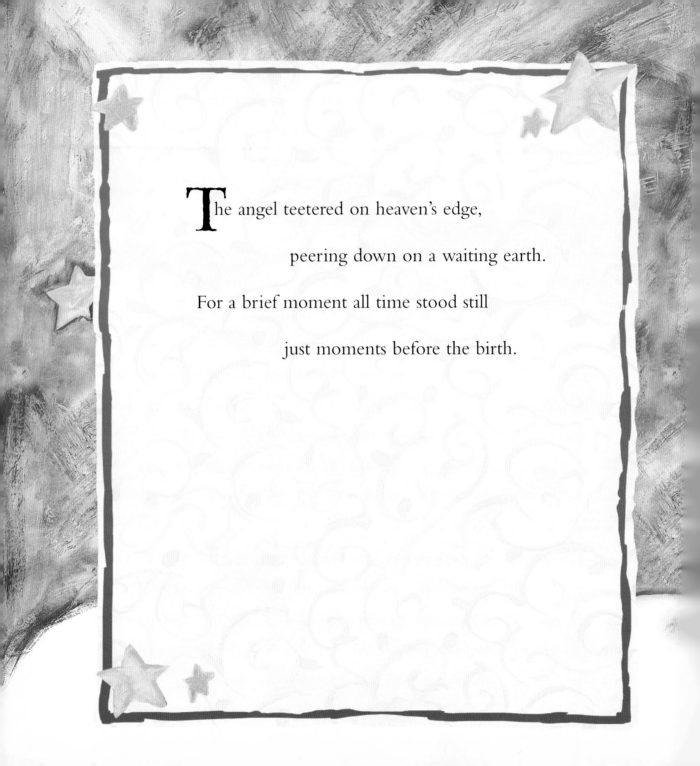

The angel teetered on heaven's edge,

peering down on a waiting earth.

For a brief moment all time stood still

just moments before the birth.

"One more thing, dear angel, before you go,"

said the Lord to His chosen one.

"Life is not always laughter and smiles . . .

not all discovery and fun.

"There will be frightening times for sure

when danger stirs alarm.

It's then you must forget all else

and protect this child from harm."

"I understand," the angel said,

"the importance of this lifelong task.

Be assured for counsel and guidance

on you I'll call and ask."

And so it was at heaven's door

as the angel prepared for flight

that God said, "Be good and do your best,"

and hugged His angel tight.

With that, the angel grabbed a star

and tumbled from on high,

touching down as earth resounded

with a baby's sweet, pure cry.

On the chosen date of *January 23, 2009*

heaven's angel witnessed the birth

of *Marin Jeanne Brooks*

God's newest blessing on earth.